LIFE

WE LEARN IN GENESIS THAT Rebekah "was very fair to look upon." One day while at the well in Nahor, Mesopotamia—here in a painting by the English artist Frederick Goodall—she met Eliezer, a servant sent by Abraham in search of a wife for his son Isaac. She accompanied Eliezer back to Canaan, married Isaac, and became a matriarch of the biblical tradition.

WOMEN OF
THE BIBLE

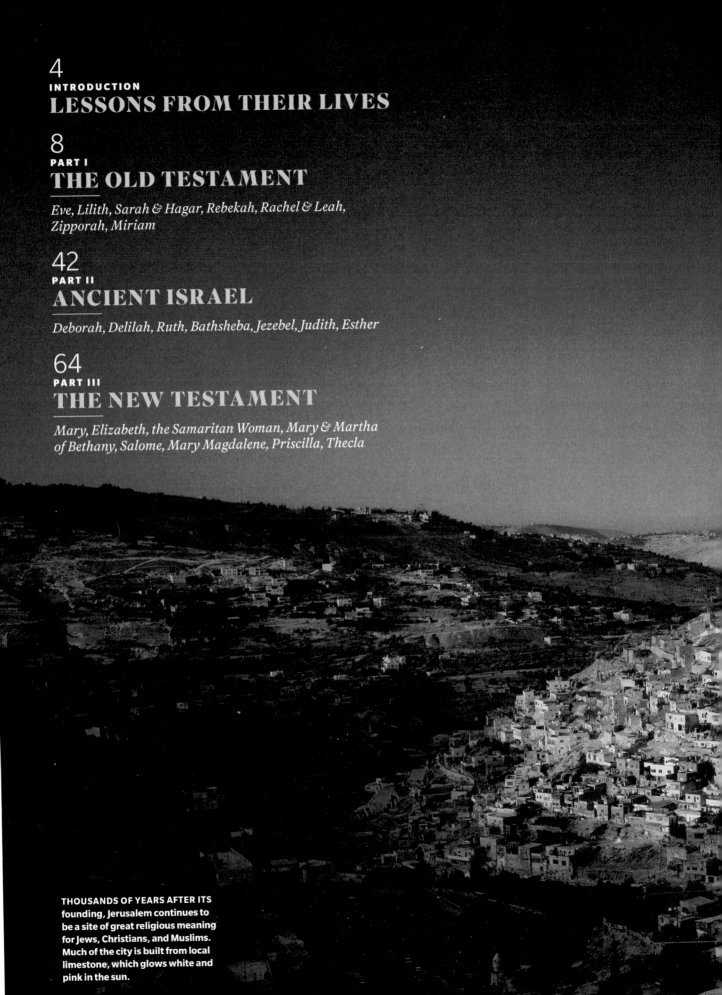

THOUSANDS OF YEARS AFTER ITS founding, Jerusalem continues to be a site of great religious meaning for Jews, Christians, and Muslims. Much of the city is built from local limestone, which glows white and pink in the sun.

LIFE

Women of the Bible

EDITORIAL DIRECTOR Kostya Kennedy
DIRECTOR OF PHOTOGRAPHY Christina Lieberman
EDITOR Lily Rothman
WRITER Daniel S. Levy
DESIGNER Allie Adams
COPY CHIEF Parlan McGaw
COPY EDITOR Helen Eisenbach
PICTURE EDITOR Rachel Hatch
WRITER-REPORTER Amy Lennard Goehner
PHOTO ASSISTANT Steph Durante
PRODUCTION DESIGN Sandra Jurevics

MEREDITH SPECIAL INTEREST MEDIA

SENIOR VICE PRESIDENT, FINANCE Anthony Palumbo
VICE PRESIDENT, MARKETING Jeremy Biloon
DIRECTOR, BRAND MARKETING Jean Kennedy
SALES DIRECTOR Christi Crowley
ASSOCIATE DIRECTOR, BRAND MARKETING Bryan Christian
ASSOCIATE DIRECTOR, FINANCE Jill Earyes
SENIOR BRAND MANAGER Katherine Barnet
EDITORIAL DIRECTOR Kostya Kennedy
CREATIVE DIRECTOR Gary Stewart
DIRECTOR OF PHOTOGRAPHY Christina Lieberman
EDITORIAL OPERATIONS DIRECTOR Jamie Roth Major
MANAGER, EDITORIAL OPERATIONS Gina Scauzillo

SPECIAL THANKS Brad Beatson, Melissa Frankenberry,
Kate Roncinske

MEREDITH NATIONAL MEDIA GROUP

PRESIDENT Jon Werther
MEREDITH MAGAZINES PRESIDENT Doug Olson
PRESIDENT, MEREDITH DIGITAL Stan Pavlovsky
PRESIDENT, CONSUMER PRODUCTS Tom Witschi
CHIEF REVENUE OFFICER Michael Brownstein
CHIEF MARKETING & DATA OFFICER Alysia Borsa
MARKETING & INTEGRATED COMMUNICATIONS Nancy Weber

SENIOR VICE PRESIDENTS

CONSUMER REVENUE Andy Wilson
DIGITAL SALES Marla Newman
RESEARCH SOLUTIONS Britta Cleveland
PRODUCT & TECHNOLOGY Justin Law
CHIEF DIGITAL OFFICER Matt Minoff
CORPORATE SALES Brian Kightlinger

VICE PRESIDENTS

FINANCE Chris Susil
BUSINESS PLANNING & ANALYSIS Rob Silverstone
DIRECT MEDIA Patti Follo
STRATEGIC SOURCING, NEWSSTAND, PRODUCTION
Chuck Howell
CONSUMER MARKETING Steve Crowe
BRAND LICENSING Steve Grune

VICE PRESIDENT, GROUP EDITORIAL DIRECTOR Stephen Orr
DIRECTOR, EDITORIAL OPERATIONS & FINANCE Greg Kayko

MEREDITH CORPORATION

PRESIDENT & CHIEF EXECUTIVE OFFICER Tom Harty
CHIEF FINANCIAL OFFICER Joseph Ceryanec
CHIEF DEVELOPMENT OFFICER John Zieser
PRESIDENT, MEREDITH LOCAL MEDIA GROUP Patrick McCreery
SENIOR VICE PRESIDENT, HUMAN RESOURCES Dina Nathanson

EXECUTIVE CHAIRMAN Stephen M. Lacy
VICE CHAIRMAN Mell Meredith Frazier

Vol. 19, No. 8 • March 15, 2019

INTRODUCTION

Lessons from Their Lives

By Lily Rothman

The narratives of the Bible are, by and large, driven by the actions and decisions of men. And yet women are always there—present and integral if frequently overlooked. If one explores the books' stories and progress, one finds that women often have a far more central role than is generally acknowledged. Women have been around just as long as men have (or almost, according to most interpretations of Genesis). Adam and Eve show up in the very same verse, just words apart from each other: Male and female, the Bible tells us, God created them.

Sometimes in Biblical stories, female figures reside in the background, unnamed or even unmentioned. Other times women emerge front and center—Deborah planning a military campaign or Salome demanding the head of John the Baptist. Often they're *very* front and *very* center: Eve deciding to eat the forbidden fruit. Mary bringing Jesus Christ into the world. This book brings these and many other women of the Bible into greater focus and relief, investigating what we know about them from the book itself, as well as

TINTORETTO'S 16TH-CENTURY depiction of the Crucifixion includes the women who supported Mary in her hour of grief (seen here in a detail).

> "Then the prophet Miriam, Aaron's sister,
> took a tambourine in her hand;
> and all the women went out after her with
> tambourines and with dancing."
>
> EXODUS, 15:20

what we have learned from modern research into the lives of the ancient peoples who lived in the Middle and Near East.

These women are sometimes heroes with superhuman-seeming bravery, risking their lives to save their people or taking decisive action to intervene in dangerous situations. At other times, they are guided by all-too-human impulses, letting jealousy rule their decisions or going to extremes to give their children an advantage over others. Terrible things happen to some of these women. Other women do terrible things themselves. Some bring wisdom, as prophets and judges. Others bring children into the world. In fact, often the critical element in a Biblical woman's story is God's intervention in the conception of a child. In this way, though constrained by circumstance and position, mothers are still active via their connection with God, a connection that moves the Biblical story forward into another generation.

RECOGNIZING THE SIGNIFICANT IMPACT OF women in Biblical narratives doesn't require glossing over the patriarchy of the societies the Bible describes—a patriarchy that, as the late theological scholar Tikva Frymer-Kensky has written, was neither created by the Bible nor repudiated by it. But as Frymer-Kensky found in her studies, the status of women in biblical society isn't necessarily accompanied by the belittling rationalizations a modern reader might expect. "On the one hand, women occupied a socially subordinate position," Frymer-Kensky wrote in *Reading the Women of the Bible*. "On the other hand, the Bible did not label them as inferior."

Nor was their influence necessarily inferior, different though it was. More subtle power of the kind that women have tended to wield throughout history can be especially important at moments of great upheaval—so much of the history recounted by the Bible.

Proof of that lasting impact is all around us in the babies everywhere who, thousands of years after the matriarchs lived, still bear their names. In the United States, Elizabeth and Leah are still among the most popular names for baby girls, according to the latest edition of the Social Security Administration's annual list of the top baby names. (Genesis has also become a popular name, though Eve is lower on the list.)

Some people have found in these Biblical stories a positive social order to replicate, in which soft power remains the only kind of power available to women. Some have found something inescapably problematic that can only be rejected. Many others have found something in between, messages to be considered and questioned. One striking example of that questioning can be seen in the development of new customs such as Miriam's Cup—a cup of water that some celebrants add to the set of ceremonial items used at the Jewish Passover holiday as a way to acknowledge the role of Miriam in the Exodus story. In telling the story of how that idea was first developed in Boston in 1989, the scholar Penina Adelman relates this observation from one of the first participants in that ritual: It felt as if the cup already existed, the woman said, "and was just waiting to be discovered."

In the pages of the Bible are many women who have been there all along. To discover them, all you have to do is look. ∎

RACHEL AND LEAH BOTH loved Jacob, but the patriarch "loved Rachel more than Leah." The sisters, seen in a 19th-century British engraving, endured a bitter rivalry as they each sought to bear the heirs Jacob desired.

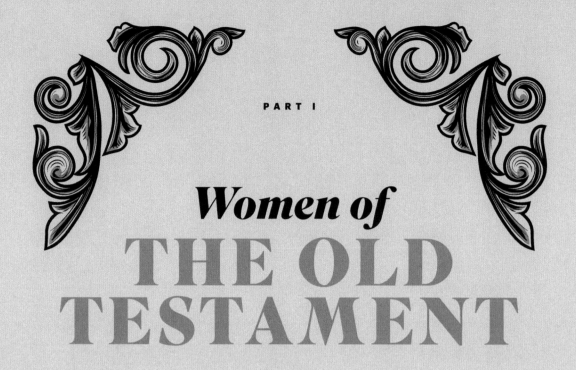

Women of
THE OLD TESTAMENT

Just as in the eternal cycles referred to in the book of Ecclesiastes, the societies of the biblical world rose and fell through wars, the pronouncements of kings, and the fickleness of gods. Over the millennia, the ancient Middle and Near East were ruled by various competing empires—the Akkadians, the Assyrians, the Egyptians, the Sumerians, the Babylonians. It was in the midst of all this, some

4,000 years ago, that a man known as Abraham lived with Sarah, his wife, in the Sumerian city of Ur.

According to the Bible, they lived about two thousand years after God created the world, though historians have found evidence of human habitation in the region stretching back much further. (The fabled city of Jericho, whose walls Joshua and his Israelite army caused to tumble down, was founded some 11,000 years ago.) We know of Abraham and Sarah's stories, and those of their descendants, primarily through the Torah, the Five Books of Moses at the heart of the Hebrew Bible, along with tantalizing clues uncovered by archaeologists sifting through the sands of Bronze Age sites and deciphering the writings from those times. Abraham's family lived near the Euphrates River in modern-day Iraq. They were originally polytheistic, probably worshipping a trinity of Sumerian deities: the moon god, Nanna; the sun god, Utu; and the goddess of war and love, Inanna. For reasons lost to history, this small clan traveled northwest to Haran, in

what today is Turkey, and then south to Canaan, in present-day Israel.

It was there that, the book of Genesis relates, God promised Abraham that "all the land that you see I will give to you and to your offspring forever."

And it was there that the first Jewish people established a toehold for monotheism, an idea that would eventually spread across the world.

Life was hard in this arid region. Even the women who were elites within this society, able to summon handmaids and slaves to do their bidding, had to be savvy survivalists, fluent in all that needed to be done, from hauling water and tending livestock to raising children and ensuring that their offspring prospered. The stories of how they did so would populate the holy books of their descendants—some of the most influential writings in history. And though the Bible is told largely from the perspective of men, their wives, sisters, daughters, and servants were an integral and essential part of the story. ■

EVE
"Mother of All Living"

TO CREATE THE FIRST HUMAN BEING, "God formed man from the dust of the ground, and breathed into his nostrils the breath of life." This creation is called Adam, which in Hebrew means both "man" and "human." This causes some scholars to interpret the reference in Genesis to mean that the first person was androgynous, but Adam is generally seen as male. God's creation cannot live alone, so God puts Adam to sleep and, using one of his ribs as raw material, creates a woman. This is Eve.

Genesis tells of how the two initially live as equals in the Garden of Eden, where all they want is taken care of. Created in God's own image, they are entrusted with stewardship over the land. In the middle of this paradise, though, stand two trees, the tree of life and the tree of knowledge of good and evil. These, God instructs the couple, cannot be touched. Yet in the midst of the newborn world, God has also set a subtle serpent who tells the woman that she should eat from the tree of knowledge. "Your eyes will be opened," the serpent promises, "and you will be like God." Eve accepts a fruit—not specifically an apple, though apples have long been associated

EVE WAS ONE OF THE TWO innocents in the Garden of Eden, and there she met a "crafty" serpent, above in a 19th-century pastel and gouache by the French symbolist artist Lucien Lévy-Dhurmer. The serpent convinced her to eat from the tree of knowledge, which led God, opposite in an engraving by the 19th-century French artist Gustave Doré, to expel her and Adam from paradise.

> "This at last is bone of my bones and flesh of my flesh; this one shall be called Woman, for out of Man this one was taken."
>
> GENESIS, 2:23

with the story—and takes a bite before giving it to Adam.

This moment would prompt millennia worth of debate. In Genesis, the woman simply hands the fruit to the man, an act that many scholars interpret as replicating the way a woman in ancient Israelite culture would have been the traditional preparer of food. The eating of the fruit, though, has been interpreted by Christians as humankind's original sin.

This disregard of God's instructions brings down the Lord's wrath. Man is destined to toil in hard and sweaty labor. And upon the woman, whom Adam had given a name meaning "mother of all living," God bestows the ability to bear children, with its attendant physical pain. The Bible also indicates in this section that man is the dominant partner, a passage that has been taken by some to indicate his right to lord over his mate. Some scholars have interpreted the wording as specific instructions for the marital bed—"your desire shall be for your husband / and he shall rule over you"—but others throughout the ages have seen in it both the cause and reflection of ideas about the role of man and woman in society and in relation to each other.

As their final punishment, the pair is banished from paradise. Outside of Eden, Eve gives birth to numerous children, the most famous being Cain, the farmer, and Abel, the shepherd, whom his brother kills; Abel's death is the first murder recorded in the Bible. When Eve and Adam are 130 years old, she gives birth to Seth, and then other "sons and daughters"—offspring who start to populate God's earth. ■

EVE HAD TWO SONS: CAIN, "a tiller of the ground," and Abel, "a keeper of sheep." God, though, favored the sacrifice from Abel. "Cain was very angry, and his countenance fell," and in a rage he slew Abel, shown here with their mother in a painting by the 19th-century Italian artist Carlo Zatti. God banished the first son, and he settled in the land of Nod, to the east of Eden.

LILITH

Lilith is a creature of Jewish folklore, mentioned by the prophet Isaiah in the 8th century BCE. She is based on the Babylonian night monster and storm demon Lilitu. Like Adam, Lilith was said to have been molded from the earth; she claimed equality with him and refused to be subservient. A cult related to Lilith lasted into the Common Era, and it was believed that she was a creature who endangered pregnant women and children, and that she used men to give birth to demons. Michelangelo seems to have included her as a redheaded half woman–half serpent temptress in the Sistine Chapel, while Irish novelist James Joyce called her in *Ulysses* the "patron of abortions." More recently, however, Lilith has been embraced by modern feminists, who see in her story a symbol of the possibility of a more equal role for women in society.

Cradle of Civilization

Four rivers flow out of the Garden of Eden: the Pishon, the Gihon, the Euphrates, and the Tigris. Some of the earliest human settlements—such as Ur, where Sarah and Abraham came from—flourished alongside the Tigris. The ancient city of Hasankeyf is 10,000 years old and contains thousands of man-made caves, medieval monuments, and many ancient ruins.

SARAH & HAGAR

The Matriarchs of Two Great Faiths

GOD'S PROMISE TO ABRAHAM IS COM-plicated: Though Abraham is to be the patriarch of his people, he had no children. His wife Sarah's barrenness is so well-established that, Genesis relates, she laughs when three strangers visit their campsite in Hebron and one of the guests says that she will have a son. God—who had, in disguise, been one of the strangers—asks Abraham why his wife laughs, given that divine power is limitless. When Sarah hears this she becomes frightened and denies laughing.

But the omniscient visitor tells her, "Oh, yes, you did laugh."

While Sarah, whose name means "princess," is beautiful and desired by both the Egyptian Pharaoh and a Philistine king, she is in her seventies by that point. The inability to bear children is a common theme in the Bible, often providing the primary obstacle in a woman's story. When God intercedes and the woman becomes pregnant, her story propels the narrative—and also gives her a way to influence the clan's future.

SARAH COULD NOT CONCEIVE a child, and she gave Abraham her Egyptian slave-girl Hagar as a wife, opposite in a 17th-century painting by the Dutch master Matthias Stom. Yet Sarah resented the attention that Hagar and Hagar's son, Ishmael, received, and after Sarah's own child, Isaac, was born, she had Abraham banish the pair, above in an oil by the German painter Johann Friedrich Overbeck.

Since Sarah could not ensure Abraham's bloodline, she gives her Egyptian slave-girl, Hagar, to him as a wife. Offering servants to husbands was a common practice. In ancient Mesopotamia some marriage contracts even contained a clause that allowed a husband to father a child with a slave if his wife did not conceive. For Hagar, Sarah's decree improves her position within the household, but her ease in that new position unnerves Sarah. When Hagar becomes pregnant, she looks down on her mistress. Sarah accuses her husband of supporting that source of unhappiness, and Abraham tells her, "Your slave-girl is in your power; do to her as you please." Sarah deals harshly with Hagar, who runs away.

As Hagar, whose name possibly means "wanderer," makes her way through the desert, she stops at a spring. There, an angel tells her to return to the encampment and promises her that her son:

"…shall be a wild ass of a man,
with his hand against everyone,
and everyone's hand against him;
and he shall live at odds with his kin."

In Hagar's response, she becomes the first person to name God, saying, "You are El-roi," which could mean either "God of seeing" or "God who sees." She dutifully returns to the encampment,

and there gives birth to Ishmael.

But God's promise to Sarah is yet to be fulfilled, that "she shall give rise to nations; kings of peoples shall come from her." When Sarah is 90, she gives birth to a son she and Abraham name Isaac, "laughter." After Sarah weans Isaac, Abraham throws a feast for him. During the party, Sarah watches as Isaac plays with his teenage half brother. She is afraid for Isaac's position in the household and insists that Abraham banish Hagar and Ishmael.

One morning, Abraham hands Hagar some bread and water and sends them away. The two wander in the wilderness.

Soon they run out of water, and Hagar puts Ishmael under a shrub and weeps knowing that he is about to die. God hears Hagar weeping, and an angel speaks to her from heaven and promises her that from Ishmael, God "will make him a great nation." Hagar then spies a well of water and they are saved. As prophesized, Ishmael grows strong. Hagar finds him an Egyptian wife, and he has 12 sons, all of whom become princes. Muhammad, the founder of Islam, descends from this lineage.

We hear nothing again of Sarah until she dies at age 127, and Abraham buries her in a cave at Machpelah. ∎

LOST IN THE WILDERNESS AND desperate for water, Hagar wept. God heard her cries, and an angel called to her, "What troubles you, Hagar?"—a scene depicted opposite in a painting by the 19th-century French painter Jean Baptiste-Camille Corot. Hagar then spied a well of water and was saved. At Hirbet es-Sibte on the West Bank stands the Oak of Mamre, seen here, which, tradition holds, marks the spot where Abraham and Sarah fed the three mysterious visitors who informed her that she would bear a child.

THE CAVE OF MACHPELAH

When Sarah dies at age 127 at Kiriath-arba—modern-day Hebron—Abraham approaches his Hittite neighbor Ephron and buys for 400 silver shekels the cave of Machpelah. There he buries Sarah. The tomb, thought to be the oldest Jewish religious site still accessible today, is the final resting place not only for her but also for Abraham, Isaac, Jacob, Rebekah, and Leah. Tradition also holds that Adam, Eve, Esau, and Jacob are interred there. During King Herod's reign (37–4 BCE), the monarch built a building over the cave. It is the only fully surviving structure from that period and has the same measurements as the sacred enclosure in Herod's temple in Jerusalem. Over the centuries the site has served as a Byzantine church and a mosque. When Israel won the Six-Day War in 1967, the building came under Israeli control. General Moshe Dayan—who led the Israeli forces to victory and was an amateur archaeologist—then undertook the first modern examination of the tomb's subterranean chamber by lowering a 12-year-old girl down with a camera. She made a map of part of the space and told of steps leading down to a small chamber.

ABRAHAM'S SERVANT, ELIEZER of Damascus, went to the city of Nahor in search of a wife for Isaac, taking with him "all kinds of choice gifts." As he stopped to water his livestock, Rebekah appeared, seen here in a painting by the 19th-century English artist Frederick Goodall. She brought Eliezer to her father's house and it was agreed that she would accompany him back to Canaan.

REBEKAH
A Determined Mother

WHEN ISAAC COMES OF AGE, ABRAHAM seeks a special bride for his son, and dispatches a servant to the land of Mesopotamia. The man soon reaches the village where Abraham's brother, Nahor, lives. The servant beseeches God to bring by the perfect woman. Before he even finishes speaking, Nahor's granddaughter, Rebekah, appears.

She is not only "very fair to look upon, a virgin," but also helps water the camels after their long journey and invites Abraham's servant to stay in her home. There the marriage pact is made, and she is given a blessing in language that, as a sign of her importance, echoes God's promise to Abraham:

"May you, our sister, become
thousands of myriads;
may your offspring gain possession
of the gates of their foes."

Rebekah makes her way to Canaan, where she marries Isaac. The Bible tells us that "he loved her," making this the first time the Bible proclaims marital love. Yet after 20 years together, Rebekah is—like her mother-in-law, Sarah—not able to conceive until God intervenes. During the difficult pregnancy that follows, God tells her that the twins she bears will grow to be two divided nations. At their birth, Isaac loves the elder, Esau, while the younger, Jacob, becomes Rebekah's favorite.

When Isaac becomes old and his

> "May you, our sister, become thousands of myriads; may your offspring gain possession of the gates of their foes."
>
> GENESIS, 24:60

vision dims, he summons Esau to receive his blessing. Yet first he tells his son to prepare a meal for him. Rebekah overhears and, intent on her youngest receiving the benediction instead, tells Jacob that she will make a meal for him to bring to his father. She then dresses Jacob in his brother's clothes and puts goatskins on him so he will feel hairy like Esau. The subterfuge works, and through Rebekah's actions Jacob receives his father's blessing—and thus inherits the mantle of leader of their people. ■

BEYOND THE TEXT
ASHERAH

The early Jews practiced monolatry, idolizing one god but allowing for the existence of many others. Hence the second commandment's formulation, "You shall have no other gods before me." One of those other deities was Asherah, "the creatress of the gods." This Canaanite mother goddess was the consort of El, the supreme god of the western Semites. Cult objects related to Asherah (left, a gold figure from the 14th century BCE) are mentioned 30 times in the Bible, and archaeological digs in the 1970s and '80s further revealed that Asherah and the deity we call God were worshipped at the same time. Then, in the 7th century BCE, the Judean king Josiah purged the temple of cult objects, and as we learn from 2 Kings, "brought out the image of Asherah from the house of the Lord . . . beat it to dust and threw the dust of it upon the graves of the common people." Soon after, the Jews were exiled to Babylon and they solidly embraced just one god.

REBEKAH LOVED HER YOUNGER son, Jacob, more than her elder, Esau. In *Isaac Blessing Jacob* by the 18th-century French painter Nicolas-Guy Brenet, the artist depicts Rebekah standing in the shadows at the entrance to the tent as Jacob—wearing "skins of the kids on his hands and on the smooth part of his neck" so his father will think he is the hairy Esau—receives his blessing.

As It Once Was

Sheep grazing in the Judean Hills outside of Bethlehem are a sight not so different from one that would have been seen in the time of the matriarchs.

RACHEL & LEAH
Two Sisters in One Fraught Household

REBEKAH AND ISAAC'S SON ESAU NOT
only loses his inheritance but he also marries two Hittite women, unions that "made life bitter for Isaac and Rebekah." His mother worries that if their other son, Jacob, whom she prefers, also makes an unsuitable marriage, things will only get worse. So Isaac sends Jacob to his uncle Laban's house in Paddan-aram in Mesopotamia to find an acceptable wife. When Jacob arrives, he comes upon his cousin Rachel by a well. He is immediately smitten by the woman, whose name means "ewe." Laban, though, does not make the courtship easy.

He first insists that his nephew work for him for seven years before a marriage will be allowed. And when the wedding day arrives, unbeknownst to Jacob, Laban switches his daughters. Instead of marrying Rachel, Jacob learns after his wedding night that he has instead married her older sister, Leah. Laban informs him that if he wants Rachel's hand, too, he needs to work for another seven years, which he dutifully does.

The Bible thus sets up what becomes a bitter co-wives-and-sisters rivalry. Because Jacob already prefers Rachel, God helps Leah and allows the "soft-eyed"

JACOB WAS IMMEDIATELY SMITTEN with Rachel, as seen opposite in the painting by the 19th-century German artist Erwin Speckter. Yet his father-in-law, Laban, tricked him into first marrying her sister, Leah. This page: At a caravanserai (a guest-house inn) in Fallujah, near where the Tigris and Euphrates rivers meet, merchants early in the last century prepared to continue on their journeys.

"Leah's eyes were lovely, and Rachel was graceful and beautiful."

GENESIS, 29:17

wife to bear children. Leah then bestows upon her sons names she hopes will touch her husband's heart: Reuben, "see, a son"; Simeon, "God heard that I am unloved"; Levi, "now my husband will be with me"; and Judah, "praise."

Not being able to bear an heir incenses Rachel, who demands of Jacob, "Give me children, or I shall die." As Sarah once did, she offers her husband her maid, Bilhah, who gives birth to Dan and then Naphtali. Not to be outdone, Leah also offers Jacob her maid, Zilpah, who bears Gad and Asher. The eldest, Reuben, then finds a much-sought-after mandrake root, which is thought to have aphrodisiac and fertility properties, which he gives to Leah, who promptly gives birth to sons Issachar and Zebulun and daughter Dinah. Finally, after Jacob already has 11 children, God "opens" Rachel's womb. She bears Joseph and proclaims that "my God has taken away my reproach."

After laboring for years for Laban, Jacob decides to take his family back to Canaan. They pass through the land where Esau lives. Because he has betrayed Esau, Jacob fears for his and his family's safety. He sends ahead a generous peace offering of livestock, but he is not sure if this will appease Esau and, just before the two meet, Jacob takes steps to protect himself. Though Esau is in fact pleased to see his brother, Jacob's strategem again reveals who is his favorite: He has set the maids and their children in front, Leah and her children next, and Rachel and Joseph shielded at the rear.

As they travel, Rachel becomes pregnant again. She endures a hard labor, and just before she dies she gives birth to a son she names Ben-oni, whom Jacob calls Benjamin. Jacob buries her along the way in Bethlehem. Later, when Leah dies, she is placed in the cave in Machpelah. ∎

JACOB WITH RACHEL, LEAH, and Laban in a painting by the 17th-century French artist Claude Lorrain. The patriarch spent two decades taking care of his father-in-law's herds. God then told Jacob, "Return to the land of your ancestors and to your kindred, and I will be with you."

RACHEL'S TOMB

When Rachel died, Jacob set up a pillar at her grave—and the site of that marker has become a pilgrimage destination for those praying for their children and seeking help becoming pregnant. It has also become a popular destination for practitioners of Kabbalah, Jewish mysticism. Many Jews and non-Jews alike believe that wearing a strand of red yarn that has been wrapped around Rachel's Tomb—the third holiest site in Judaism—will protect the wearer from *ayin hara,* the evil eye. In recent years such strands have been seen on the wrists of celebrities from Mick Jagger to Ivanka Trump. One well-known student of Kabbalah is Madonna. Her 2004 visit to the tomb required more than 1,000 police officers to protect her from protesters— both Palestinians, who regard the site as a mosque, and Orthodox Jews, many of whom find the Catholic-born singer's study of Kabbalah insensitive.

ZIPPORAH
Quick-Thinking Wife

AS WITH RACHEL AND JACOB, ZIPPORAH meets her future husband, Moses, alongside a well. By this point in the book of Exodus, the Israelites have spent centuries enslaved in Egypt, and Jacob and Joseph are long dead. Moses has fled that land, and when arriving in Midian in the Sinai and northern Arabia, he stops to rest at that well. There, he defends the seven daughters of Jethro, the local priest, from a group of shepherds. In gratitude, Jethro offers Moses his daughter Zipporah—whose name means "bird"—as a bride. Moses starts to tend his father-in-law's flock and the couple has two sons, Gershom and Eliezer.

It is while Moses is watching Jethro's sheep that God is revealed to him in the burning bush, convincing Moses to return with Zipporah to Egypt to save their people. Along the way, one of the Bible's more unexplained events occurs. One night God tries to kill Moses, perhaps out of displeasure that Moses has not circumcised his sons. Zipporah leaps to her husband's defense, performing the rite on one of the boys and then touching Moses's feet with the foreskin, saying, "Truly you are a *hatan* of blood to me!" The Hebrew word used in the passage can mean either father-in-law or bridegroom, so it is not clear if she is referring to Moses or God. Either way, the group is allowed to live.

After Moses leads the Israelites out of the desert, he sends Zipporah and his sons back to Jethro. Though the family is later reunited, Moses essentially ignores his wife, possibly because of an injunction against sex for men who are awaiting God. Since Moses is continuously at God's beck and call, he cannot stay with her. ■

AS ZIPPORAH AND MOSES headed back to Egypt, God attacked Moses. Zipporah saved her husband by circumcising one of their sons, as seen in this painting by the 17th-century Dutch artist Jan Baptist Weenix. Soon after, they met up with Moses's brother, Aaron, and set out to free their people.

Hard Service in Mortar and Brick

The pyramids of Giza are but a few of the many structures built by the Pharaohs of Egypt. The Israelites spent centuries in the kingdom along the Nile and constructed the "supply cities, Pithom and Rameses, for Pharaoh." In the book of Exodus, God tells Moses to confront Pharaoh, and warns, "Now you shall see what I will do to Pharaoh."

MIRIAM
The First Female Prophet

MOST OF THE WOMEN IN THE BIBLE are defined as wives or daughters, but there are exceptions—among them, Miriam, Moses's sister. It is she who watches over the small basket in which their mother, Jochebed, sets baby Moses afloat among the bulrushes of the Nile after the Pharaoh orders the death of every male child of the Hebrews. And it is Miriam who tells the Pharaoh's daughter, who discovers the basket, that she knows of a wet nurse to care for the child, thus ensuring that Jochebed can tend to her son. And it is Miriam who, after God parts the waters of the Red Sea, and the Jews escape Egypt, leads the celebration. In the passage, Miriam "took a tambourine in her hand; and all the women went out after her with tambourines and with dancing."

Linguistic studies of the Song of Miriam and of the longer, preceding Song of Moses have shown that the passages are written in an archaic version of Hebrew that predates the rest of Exodus. Early copies that were found in the Dead Sea Scrolls, which were discovered in the last century, attributed the entire song to Miriam. "She is a strong and an enigmatic figure. It is possible that she was a

THE FINDING OF MOSES, BY the 20th-century British artist Harry Mileham, shows the moment when the Egyptian princess discovered the infant Moses floating in his basket, below. Miriam fetched their mother, Jochebed, to serve as a nurse for the baby, as depicted opposite by the Pre-Raphaelite painter Simeon Solomon.

AS THE ISRAELITES FLED, GOD parted the Red Sea and then destroyed the pursuing Egyptians, as depicted here in a painting by the 19th-century Irish artist Francis Danby. With their enemy vanquished, Miriam led the women of Israel in celebration, seen below in Simeon Solomon's *The Song of Miriam*.

lot stronger than the Bible tells us," says Professor Carol Meyers, author of *Discovering Eve: Ancient Israelite Women in Context,* noting evidence that those who put together the various books of the Bible toned down her influence. "But she was so important that they couldn't write her out completely."

During the 40 years that the Jews spend in the desert after their escape, the three siblings lead their people. Even though Miriam appears less often than her brothers do, she is still integral. She is called in the Bible "the prophet Miriam," the first woman to bear that designation. In the book of Numbers, though, when the Jews are in Hazeroth, Miriam and Aaron become angry at Moses and challenge his leadership of their group, reminding him that God has spoken through them as well.

To settle the breach, God summons the three of them and, after descending in a pillar of clouds, clearly makes it known that Moses is in charge. As God departs, only Miriam is punished, not Aaron, and she becomes "leprous, as white as snow." Both brothers fear for their sister, and Moses cries out to God to heal Miriam. After God instructs Moses to set Miriam outside the camp for a week, the Israelites refuse to continue until she is cured.

When Miriam later dies, the world seems to mourn, and the water sources dry up. ■

MIRIAM'S CUP

During the Passover Seder, the ceremonial meal at which Jews celebrate the Exodus, it is traditional to set out a plate of items that represent parts of the story. A cup of wine is also set out for Elijah, the prophet who will herald the Messiah. Many modern celebrants have added a cup for Miriam. Miriam's Cup contains water, for she watched over baby Moses at the Nile, she was there when the Red Sea parted, and Miriam's Well supplied the Israelites with water in the desert. Some Orthodox Jews have similarly revived a custom of placing a fish on the Seder plate to acknowledge her. The Babylonian Talmud, which contains commentaries on the Bible, stresses the importance of women in the Exodus story, declaring, "If it wasn't for the righteousness of women of that generation we would not have been redeemed from Egypt."

WHEN THE ISRAELITES ARRIVED AT Jericho, Joshua's warriors and seven priests circled the city with the Ark of the Covenant for seven days. On the final day, Joshua commanded all his people to shout. As they raised their voices, "the wall fell down flat," as illustrated in a fresco at the Vatican.

PART II

Women of ANCIENT ISRAEL

Though the Israelites had escaped from Egyptian slavery, the period of history that follows the Book of Exodus was still one of great turmoil. In this time, covered by the rest of the Hebrew Bible—which is made up of the books of Nevi'im (Prophets) and Ketuvim (Writings)—the Jewish people completed their transformation from the clan of families led by the matriarchs and patriarchs into a civilization.

It was Joshua who brought the Jews into the "land flowing with milk and honey." With God's help, they conquered the territory and divided it among the 12 tribes of Israel. After Joshua's death, judges like Deborah led that confederation, until the people told the Prophet Samuel they were "determined to have a king over us." Around 1020 BCE, Samuel elevated the military leader Saul to the throne. His successor David captured the city of Jerusalem, placing there the Ark of the Covenant—the sacred container of the Ten Commandments—thus linking David's capital, his anointed dynasty, and the shrine of God.

Solomon, David's son with Bathsheba, constructed a temple in Jerusalem. Trade flourished, much of it through colonies, treaties, and his 700 marriages. The 10 northern tribes split off after Solomon's death and formed the Kingdom of Israel, while the tribes of Judah and Benjamin made up the Kingdom of Judah.

Both proved ineffective. Around 720 BCE the Assyrians conquered the north, and those tribes vanished from history. Then in 586 the Babylonian king Nebuchadnezzar destroyed Solomon's temple and deported part of the Judean population. It was only when the Persian king Cyrus II defeated the Babylonians in 538 BCE that the Jews returned, and began building a new temple.

Peace, though, would not hold. Alexander the Great conquered Israel in 332, and soon Hellenized beliefs spread. When in the second century BCE the Seleucid king Antiochus IV Epiphanes outlawed Jewish practices, the Maccabee family revolted and established the Hasmonean dynasty. Seeking to hold onto power, some of the Hasmoneans sought help from Rome, and by 63 BCE the territory promised to Abraham had become a client kingdom of that empire.

Throughout, the women of that civilization played important roles—sometimes from positions of power but more frequently by exerting what subtle influence they could. ■

DEBORAH, IN THIS PAINTING by Francesco Solimena, commanded Barak to gather his troops for battle. Opposite: The Plain of Jezreel, where the rain brought by God caused Sisera's chariots to stick in the mud.

DEBORAH
A Victorious Judge

AFTER JOSHUA'S DEATH, 15 JUDGES lead the tribes of Israel; only one is a woman. Deborah holds court in the hill town of Ephraim, listening to cases while sitting under what was known as Deborah's Palm Tree. In Hebrew she is called *eshet lapidot,* which can either mean "wife of Lappidoth," her husband's name, or "woman of torches," since she prepares the wicks in the tabernacle. She is a prophet in the book of Judges, and is also called "Mother of Israel."

At the time, the 12 tribes have a fierce enemy in the Canaanite king Jabin of Hazor and his fearsome general Sisera. The Israelites beg God for help, and the Lord tells Deborah to order a man named Barak to gather warriors for a fight. Barak, though, is reluctant. "If you will go with me, I will go; but if you will not go with me, I will not go," he says to her. Deborah responds, "I will surely go with you." And, she tells him, he will not be the one to secure the victory, for "the Lord will sell Sisera into the hand of a woman."

Deborah plots her campaign. She plans to draw out Sisera's chariots and troops, and tells Barak where she will deliver the enemy into his hands. Sure enough, God is clearly on the Israelite's side and "the earth trembled, and the heavens poured, the clouds indeed poured water," disabling the chariots.

Terrified, the Canaanites flee and are struck down. Only Sisera escapes, finding a hiding place in the tent of a woman named Jael, wife of Heber the Kenite. The Kenites are a tribe related to Jethro—Moses's father-in-law—and are allies of the Israelites. Jael hides him under a rug. When Sisera asks for water, Jael pours him some warm milk, which relaxes him. After he dozes off, she takes a tent peg and drives it through his skull. Thanks to the actions of a woman, just as Deborah had predicted, the Israelites soon overthrow King Jabin and enjoy 40 years of peace. ■

DELILAH
The Philistine Temptress

THE ISRAELITES' NEIGHBORS FROM THE land of Philistia have good reason to fear Samson, the longhaired Israelite warrior-judge. Once, in a rage, he slew 1,000 of them with merely the jawbone of a donkey. The Philistines set out to discover the source of his superhuman strength. One thing they know is that while he is a Nazarite—a sacred person who abstains from alcohol—Samson has a weakness for Philistine women, especially one called Delilah. Hoping to discover his frailty, the rulers of the main Philistine cities each offer Delilah, whose name means "flirtatious," 1,100 pieces of silver to learn his secret. "Coax him, and find out what makes his strength so great," they tell her, "and how we may overpower him, so that we may bind him in order to subdue him."

Delilah first questions Samson directly. He tells her numerous ways to overpower him. But each time one is tried, Samson easily breaks his bonds. Undeterred, Delilah continues to implore him, "How can you say, 'I love you,' when your heart is not with me?" Finally Samson admits that his power comes from the fact that he has never cut his hair.

So, as Delilah cradles a sleeping Samson's head on her lap, she has seven locks of his hair cut off. The Philistines rush in, capture him, and gouge out his eyes. To rejoice, they make a sacrifice to their god Dagon. As they celebrate, Samson begs God to give him back his strength one last time. Then, grasping two pillars, the blind Samson pulls down the building and crushes 3,000 men and women. Whether Delilah is one of them goes unmentioned. ∎

THE JUDGE SAMSON COULD NOT resist the allure of the Philistine woman Delilah, as seen in a painting by the Spanish artist José Echenagusia Errazquin, opposite. After Samson revealed to her that his strength came from his uncut hair, his power—as shown in this oil by the Dutch painter Gerrit van Honthorst—was snipped away.

RUTH

The Embracer of a New Heritage

IN MOAB, THE LAND TO THE EAST OF the Dead Sea, a woman named Ruth lives with her Jewish husband, whom she met after he settled there with his parents and brothers. But after all the men of the family die, Ruth's mother-in-law, Naomi, decides to return to Judea. Rather than stay in Moab, Ruth says to her:

"Where you go, I will go;
where you lodge, I will lodge;
your people shall be my people,
and your God my God.
Where you die, I will die."

The book of Ruth, like the book of Exodus, deals with exile and return. Clearly devoted to her husband's family and their beliefs, Ruth heads to Bethlehem with Naomi. In need of food, they by chance—or possibly because of divine intervention—come to a barley field belonging to Boaz, one of Naomi's deceased husband's relatives. He likes Ruth, allows her to glean the fields, and advises his servants to leave extra grain behind for her. On Naomi's advice, and in need of a husband, Ruth goes to see Boaz after the harvest. When he falls asleep, she lies down with him. Society views him as a "redeeming kinsman," a man who has the right to help and even in some cases marry a relative's widow, and soon they wed. Ruth then gives birth to a son, Obed, the grandfather of King David. She is later listed in the book of Matthew as an ancestor of Jesus. Jews read her story at Shavuot, the harvest festival, during which they celebrate the giving of the Torah to Moses at Mount Sinai. ■

AFTER THE WIDOW RUTH MOVED to Bethlehem, she realized that Boaz was interested in her and she rested with him on the threshing floor, as seen, opposite, in a painting by British artist Charles Lock Eastlake. The couple wed—here, in an Italian baroque painting by Ciro Ferri— and the citizens proclaimed, "May the Lord make the woman who is coming into your house like Rachel and Leah, who together built up the house of Israel."

Guarding a Holy City

The Tower of David was constructed in the 8th century BCE by King Hezekiah, a descendent of the great Israelite monarch. Hezekiah set it on the highest point in Jerusalem to protect the city from the expected attack of King Sennacherib of Assyria.

BATHSHEBA
A Queen Who Becomes a Kingmaker

IN THE TIME OF KING DAVID, URIAH THE Hittite is a warrior hero, off fighting the king's enemies while his king is home resting. It is during one of those wars that David takes a stroll along the roof of his palace and spies Uriah's wife, Bathsheba, bathing. Stunned by her beauty, David has her brought to him and sleeps with her. Bathsheba soon sends David word that she is pregnant. When Uriah returns, David hopes that he will spend time with his wife and think the child is his own. When that doesn't happen, David sends Uriah back to battle and tells a commander to ensure that he dies there.

The text of the story sets the blame for adultery and Uriah's death squarely on David's shoulders. The prophet Nathan upbraids the king, telling him that God "will raise up trouble against you from within your own house." Even so, David and Bathsheba marry. After the son born of their adultery dies, Bathsheba gives birth to Solomon and later to Shammua, Shobab, and Nathan, just a few of David's many children with his assorted wives and concubines. And as the prophet prophesied, trouble grows. David's daughter Tamar is raped by his son Amnon, who is killed by another one of his sons, Absalom, who then dies as he leads a revolt against their father.

All this filicide and fratricide clears the way for Solomon to succeed. The only thing standing between him and the throne is his half brother Adonijah. And while Bathsheba might have been passive at the start, she now becomes a kingmaker. With Nathan's help, she convinces the dying David that Solomon should reign. Having lost the throne, Adonijah hopes for a consolation prize in the form of one of his father's concubines. Though Bathsheba agrees to help with this plan, she intentionally relays his message in a way that angers Solomon, who has Adonijah executed. ∎

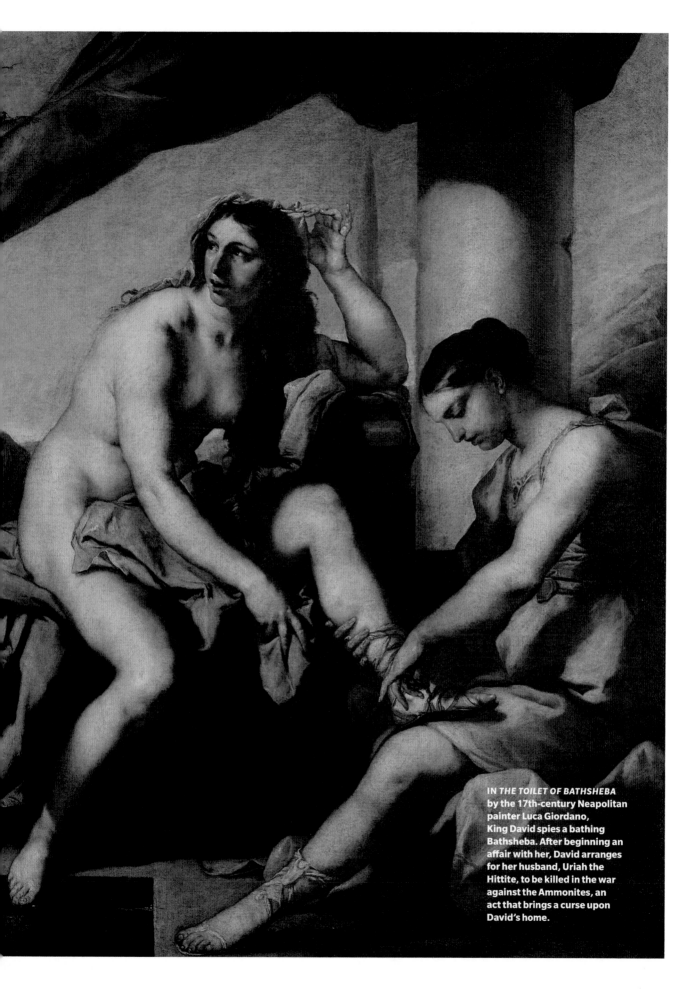

IN *THE TOILET OF BATHSHEBA* by the 17th-century Neapolitan painter Luca Giordano, King David spies a bathing Bathsheba. After beginning an affair with her, David arranges for her husband, Uriah the Hittite, to be killed in the war against the Ammonites, an act that brings a curse upon David's home.

JEZEBEL
Israel's Idol-Worshipping Queen

JEZEBEL IS THE DAUGHTER OF THE Phoenician king Ethbaal, and her name has become synonymous with that of the wicked woman. She marries Ahab, ruler of the Northern kingdom in the 9th century BCE, but when she arrives in his capital she brings hundreds of prophets of the god Baal and the goddess Asherah. Moreover, as they set up shrines to their foreign gods, Jezebel slaughters all Israelite prophets who oppose her.

This invokes the wrath of Elijah. The great Hebrew prophet predicts that Jezebel's actions will bring about a major drought. Three parched years later, when Elijah announces that God will end the dry spell, he challenges the pagan priests to see whose god could start a fire to sacrifice a bull. The pagan priests fail, while the fire of the God of the Israelites falls from the sky and consumes not only the offering but also the dust and the stones around it. After this, the Israelites kill the opposing clergy and heavy rains then begin to fall. But Elijah's execution of the pagan priests infuriates Jezebel, and he has to flee when he learns of her desire to murder him, a clear sign of the fear she instills throughout the kingdom.

When Elijah hears that Jezebel has caused a man to be stoned to death because he would not sell his vineyard to King Ahab, the prophet places a curse on Ahab. The king dies fighting the Syrians, some time after which the commander Jehu ascends to the throne. He kills Jezebel's son and has the palace eunuchs hurl her from a window. Dogs then devour her corpse. ■

JEZEBEL WAS A VAIN QUEEN OF the Northern Kingdom, seen in a painting by John Byam Liston Shaw, opposite. Born in Phoenicia, Jezebel brought with her pagan worship. Following the death of her husband, King Ahab, King Jehu had palace eunuchs defenestrate her, as depicted here in *The Death of Jezebel* by the baroque painters Giovanni Coli and Filippo Gherardi.

JUDITH
A Courageous Widow

IN THE BOOK OF JUDITH—WHICH IS part of the Apocrypha, volumes not included in the official canon—the heroine uses her cunning to save her hometown, Bethulia. King Nebuchadnezzar has sent his general Holofernes to attack the Israelites. He lays siege to Judith's city, and eventually the local magistrate proclaims that if God does not rescue them in five days, they will surrender. Incensed that the town leaders want to bargain with God, Judith says, "Do not try to bind the purposes of the Lord our God; for God is not like a human being, to be threatened, or like a mere mortal, to be won over by pleading."

Seeing that the men of the community continue to do nothing, Judith implores God, "Give to me, a widow, the strong hand to do what I plan." She then heads to the enemy's encampment, saying she has news for the general and that she will help his forces. Holofernes, taken by Judith's beauty, invites her to a banquet. Before arriving, she makes sure "to dress herself in all her woman's finery." When Holofernes sees her, his "heart was ravished with her and his passion was aroused, for he had been waiting for an opportunity to seduce her from the day he first saw her." They dine, during which the general has "much more than he had ever drunk in any one day." He promptly falls asleep. Judith takes his sword and strikes his neck "twice with all her might" and cuts off his head.

Judith then brings Holofernes's head to the townspeople of Bethulia, who set it on the city's parapets. Inspired by Judith's bravery, the people rally and defeat the enemy. ■

SEEKING TO LIFT THE SIEGE on her hometown, Bethulia, Judith made her way to the encampment of General Holofernes. There she beguiled him and lopped off his head, carrying it in victory back to Bethulia, as depicted in the inlay by Lorenzo Lotto, opposite, and this oil by Artemisia Gentileschi.

ESTHER
Protector of Persia's Jews

LIKE JUDITH, ESTHER CUNNINGLY finds a way to help her people. Born in Persia during the Babylonian exile, Esther is raised by her cousin Mordecai. The short book of Esther is one of only two in the Bible that is named for a woman, one of the few that takes place outside of Israel, and one of only two that do not mention the name of God.

When the Persian king Ahasuerus banishes his wife, Vashti, because she refuses to appear at a grand banquet to "show the peoples and the officials her beauty," a contest is announced to find

him a new spouse. Mordecai convinces Esther to enter. She is a great beauty, and when Ahasuerus lays eyes on her, "the king loved Esther more than all the other women" and so she becomes his queen.

After Esther ascends to the throne, Ahasuerus's grand vizier, Haman, becomes incensed that Mordecai refuses to bow down to him. Haman, unaware of Mordecai's relationship to the queen, sets out not only to kill Mordecai but to exterminate all the Jews. Mordecai asks Esther for her help. Despite the danger, she resolves to reveal her heritage to her

IN PREPARATION FOR A BEAUTY contest being held to find a new queen, Esther, seen above being attended to in a painting by Edwin Long, received a treatment of "six months with oil of myrrh and six months with perfumes and cosmetics for women." As queen, opposite, in an engraving by Gustave Doré, she denounced Haman and stopped the slaughter of her people.

husband. Esther invites Ahasuerus and Haman to dinner. When the king offers her anything she desires, she simply requests, "let my life be given me—that is my petition—and the lives of my people—that is my request." Alarmed, the king asks who seeks to harm her. Esther then points to "this wicked Haman," whom the king summarily orders hanged. And while Ahasuerus cannot revoke his decree against the Jews, he issues another one that allows the Jews to defend themselves. On the day of the pogrom, instead of being slaughtered, the Jews instead kill 75,000 of their enemies, including Haman's 10 sons.

Despite the danger and violence that Esther and her people endure, this brave queen's story would prove encouraging for those in exile. From it evolved the Jewish festival of Purim, a joyous day to read of Esther's heroics, dress up as characters from the book, and eat delicacies like hamantaschen, a triangular pastry that is said to be shaped like Haman's hat. ∎

THE SHORT BOOK OF ESTHER is written in a form that is called a *megillah,* on a scroll with a single wooden shaft, as distinct from the double rollers used for the longer books of the Bible. During the Purim holiday, it is read in synagogues from the parchment scroll, like the 18th-century illuminated version below.

ESTHER'S TOMB

Before the 1979 revolution there, Iran had a vibrant Jewish community of some 100,000. In the western city of Hamadan stands the tomb of Esther and Mordecai. The original tomb was destroyed in the 14th century, and the current domed brick structure was built at the start of the 17th century. Legend has it that there is an entrance there to a tunnel that leads to Jerusalem, a thousand miles away. Though it has been suggested that the tomb actually contains the 5th-century remains of Queen Shushandokht, the Jewish wife of King Yazdegerd (it was she who gave permission for Jews to live in Hamadan), the site has long served as a popular Purim pilgrimage destination. Iranian Jews have traditionally visited the tomb to read the *megillah*— the single scroll containing the book of Esther—as well as to get married and celebrate Bar Mitzvahs.

Only 9,000 Jews remain in Iran, living under a regime that heavily persecutes them. And while the chapel still has a skylight shaped like a Star of David, Iranian authorities removed its gate because it contained the same symbol. In 2011, militants threatened to tear down the building after the state news agency stoked anti-Semitism by reporting that Esther and Mordecai had long ago caused the massacre of 75,000 Iranians.

Fit for a King

The Persian palace of Persepolis was built by Darius I, father of Xerxes I. Also known as Ahasuerus, Xerxes I was the husband of Esther. He invaded Greece in the 5th century BCE and burned the Parthenon. When Alexander set out to conquer the world a century and a half later, he captured Persepolis and destroyed the royal palace.

FOLLOWING THE BIRTH OF JESUS, Herod ordered the killing of all boys two years old and under in Bethlehem. Families fled with their children, as in this painting by 19th-century French artist Leon Cogniet.

PART III

Women of
THE NEW TESTAMENT

For Rome, Israel was merely a small part of a sprawling empire. To oversee the region, Julius Caesar in 47 BCE appointed Antipater to govern Judea as its Procurator. The Edomite chieftain then founded the Herodian dynasty, and his son Herod I was proclaimed king in 37 BCE. The Edomites descended from Esau—Sarah's grandson—and had been converted to Judaism in the second century BCE.

Nevertheless, Herod's subjects viewed their king as an interloper. To appease them and impress Rome, Herod began a series of projects that included the expansion of the Temple into a grand complex with nine gates that the Roman Jewish historian Flavius Josephus said were "completely overlaid with gold and silver."

Pilgrims flocked there—including, around 4 BCE, Joseph and Mary, who had given birth to their son Jesus about a month earlier in Bethlehem. They had possibly come to take part in a ceremony for the redemption of the firstborn. But when Herod learned of the arrival of a child who was foretold to be the future King of the Jews, he feared for his throne. According to the book of Matthew, he ordered the slaughter of all babies two and under in the area around Bethlehem. Mary, Joseph, and Jesus fled to Egypt and stayed until Herod's death.

Then, around the year 30 CE, Jesus began his ministry, accompanied by his 12 disciples, as well as such women as Mary Magdalene and his mother.

They faithfully supported the group, watched the Romans crucify Jesus, and after his resurrection performed missionary work. And starting around 70 CE, the four Gospels—Matthew, Mark, Luke, and John—began to appear.

There was no uniformity of belief at the start of the church, as several sects disagreed about how best to follow the man they revered as the Messiah. Roman rulers, though, cared little for either Judaism or proto-Christianity. A massacre of Jews in the year 66 CE prompted the First Jewish Revolt. In response, in 70 CE Emperor Vespasian's elder son, Titus, destroyed Jerusalem and the Temple. With the loss of the Temple, Judaism transformed from a religion centered on sacrifices made at that sacred site to one focused on prayer and law. Synagogues became the center of Jewish religious life, while leaders such as Peter, Paul, and James helped spread what became Christianity, with its transcendent belief that redemption came through the death and resurrection of Jesus Christ. ■

MARY

The Madonna, Born Immaculately Pure

THE TEENAGE MARY LEADS AN UN-eventful life in the sleepy town of Nazareth near the Sea of Galilee. She is the daughter of an older couple, Anne and Joachim, and is betrothed to Joseph. Betrothal—which is called *erusin* in Hebrew—is the first step in a two-part Jewish marriage process. So while Mary and Joseph are legally married, she still lives with her parents prior to the *nissuin*, the wedding.

One day the angel Gabriel appears to the Nazarene and, in what is known as the Annunciation, informs her she will have a son named Jesus and he will be known as Son of God. Mary protests that she cannot have a child since she is a virgin, to which Gabriel responds that for God nothing is impossible. An angel similarly convinces Joseph not to end his relationship with Mary after he learns of her pregnancy. The two complete their nuptials and, while they are traveling through Bethlehem, she gives birth to Jesus in a stable there.

When Jesus is 12, Mary and Joseph take him to Jerusalem for the Passover celebration. The city is packed with pilgrims and, as they leave, the parents notice their son is not with them. They

MARY IS ONE OF THE MOST painted figures in history, as with the portrait of her by Carlo Maratta, opposite. In *The Wedding of Saint Mary* by the 17th-century Italian artist Luca Girodano, townspeople and heavenly hosts witness her and Joseph's sacred nuptials.

search all over town for the boy, only to finally discover Jesus at the Temple discussing Torah. When Mary lets him know that they had worried for him, Jesus answers cryptically, "Did you not know that I must be in my Father's house?"

Mary next appears at the start of Jesus's ministry, by which time he is already traveling the land, healing the sick, and preaching to those who will listen. Joseph is no longer mentioned, so it is possible that Mary is a widow when she attends a wedding in the town of Cana near Nazareth. Partway through the ceremony, the celebrants run out of wine. She informs Jesus what has happened and encourages him to perform

what would be his first miracle. Annoyed, he says that the time hasn't arrived for him to reveal who he really is. But Mary ignores her son's tone, turns to the servants and tells them to do whatever Jesus tells them to do. Jesus directs them to fill stone jars with water, and the liquid miraculously turns into fine wine.

Her son's ministry lasts but a few years. When Jesus heads to Jerusalem with his apostles for Passover in 33 CE, Mary accompanies him. There, Judas Iscariot betrays him, and most of the disciples flee. But Mary—along with Mary Magdalene, Mary of Clopas, and the disciple John—stays with him. At a place called Golgotha, which means "place of the skull," they watch in horror as Roman soldiers nail

Jesus to a cross. Just before he dies, he entrusts his mother's care to John.

Mary last appears in the book of Acts. It's not clear where she went after the death of Jesus, though some believe she traveled with John to Ephesus, Turkey, where the faithful established one of the seven branches of the church that is mentioned in the book of Revelation. And it is in Ephesus that Christians built the Church of Mary, which is believed to be the first church dedicated to her.

Because of her special position as Jesus's mother and first disciple, Christians have long accorded her special respect. The Catholic Church has four dogmas relating to Mary: the belief that she is the Mother of God, the Immaculate Conception, her Perpetual Virginity, and the Assumption. And while Catholic saints are accorded a form of veneration called *cultus dulia*, Mary has earned an even higher form of reverence, called *hyperdulia*. Because of her importance, people have long beseeched her as the Mediatrix, who offers help by interceding between humanity and God. ■

THE MARRIAGE OF CANA, below, is by the German artist Julius Schnorr von Carolsfeld, who belonged to a group of 19th-century painters who called themselves the Nazarenes and believed their work should embody religious purposes. As Jesus was taken down from the cross, Mary suffered the sixth of her seven sorrows, most famously depicted in Michelangelo's *Pietà*, opposite, created when the artist was 23.

MARY'S HOME IN EPHESUS alongside the Aegean is visited by the faithful. There they make wishes at a spring that is claimed to have curative powers, and attach precious possessions to a Wishing Wall. Opposite: At the Tomb of Mary, a staircase built by the Crusaders leads down to the crypt.

MARY'S TOMB

It is not certain where and when Mary died. She was about 50 at the time of Jesus's crucifixion, and after his death a community of his followers cared for her, so she could have lived for many more years. The Catholic and Eastern Orthodox churches both aver that she was assumed directly into heaven; the Catholic Church holds that the Assumption happened while she was alive, and the Orthodox that it happened following her demise. At Jerusalem's Mount of Olives stands the Tomb of Mary, said to have been her last resting place before she entered heaven. It is a Christian shrine as well as a spot revered by Muslims.

It is also believed that Mary spent time in Ephesus, in Turkey, having gone there with John to spread the Gospel. An early Christian community had formed in the area, and Mary is said to have lived in a small cottage (opposite), a place that has long been revered as the Doorway to the Holy Virgin, where pilgrims flock for the Feast of the Assumption.

ELIZABETH
Mary's Kin and Mother of St. John the Baptist

ELIZABETH, A RELATIVE OF MARY'S, lives in a Judean hill town with her husband, Zechariah. According to the Book of Luke, she is a descendent of Moses's brother, Aaron, and both she and her husband are "righteous before God." Yet like Sarah, Elizabeth has difficulty getting pregnant. As with many others before them in the Bible, they pray for a child. One day while Zechariah is serving as a priest in a local synagogue, the angel Gabriel appears to him. The angel tells him, "Your prayer has been heard. Your wife Elizabeth will bear you a son, and you will name him John." This child, he is told, "will turn many of the people of Israel to the Lord their God."

Elizabeth becomes pregnant, and stays in seclusion for five months, happy that God "looked favorably on me and took away the disgrace I have endured among my people."

When Elizabeth is six months pregnant, the angel Gabriel visits Mary to tell her that she will bear God's child. He also mentions Elizabeth's pregnancy, and Mary rushes to see her. As Mary greets her, Elizabeth's "child leaped in her womb," and Elizabeth realizes the importance of the child Mary will bear. Soon, Elizabeth gives birth to a boy who will become John the Baptist, who starts his own ministry in Judea and will be the one to baptize Jesus. ■

WHEN MARY LEARNED OF Elizabeth's pregnancy, she rushed to visit her, as we see in the above painting by Vittore Carpaccio. In the work opposite, by the 17th-century French painter Simon Vouet, cousins John and Jesus play between their mothers, Elizabeth and Mary, while Saint Catherine of Alexandria—who symbolizes martyrdom—looks on. The group is watched by a lamb that refers to the Passion of Christ.

DURING HIS MINISTRY, JESUS traveled from Judea back to Galilee, stopping in the Samaritan city called Sychar. There he met a Samaritan woman. The two discussed faith, as seen in this painting by the 19th-century Polish artist Henryk Siemiradzki. After they spoke, she went to the city and told the citizens about Jesus.

THE SAMARITAN WOMAN
The Open-Hearted Stranger

THE BIBLE IS FILLED WITH MANY strong women whose names are familiar, such as Deborah and Esther and Mary, but there are even more women who go unnamed. Most lived simple lives and were given such names as Weaving Woman, Pregnant Women Killed in War, Singing Woman Who Laments, and Mothers Who Agree to Eat Their Sons.

In 2 Kings, the Great Woman of Shunem appears. She lives during the time of the Prophet Elisha and is an independent woman who makes the decisions in her household, directly asks the king for what she needs, and refuses to go through intermediaries to get Elisha to resurrect her son. And in 2 Samuel, there's the Wise Woman of Abel of Beth-maacah. At the time of Absalom's failed revolt, turmoil sweeps through David's kingdom, and the Wise Woman's town is under attack. Rather than wait out the war, she negotiates with the general. "She has acumen [and] wisdom, and she helps save a city when there is this war between the people of Judah and the people of Israel," Carol Meyers, a professor of religion at Duke University, tells LIFE. "She was kind of like a psychologist. She could figure out

> "Many Samaritans from that city believed in him because of the woman's testimony, 'He told me everything I have ever done.'"
>
> JOHN, 4:39

WHEN JESUS ARRIVED IN THE district of Tyre and Sidon, an unnamed Canaanite woman approached him, shouting, "Have mercy on me, Lord, Son of David; my daughter is tormented by a demon." Though the woman was not Jewish, Jesus realized that she believed, and he responded, "Woman, great is your faith! Let it be done for you as you wish." And her daughter was healed instantly.

how to do something without violence. A peaceful leader, someone who uses diplomacy instead of force."

Jesus encounters one of these unnamed women—known as the Samaritan Woman—at a time when he is preaching in the city of Sychar, near Mount Gerizim. The Samaritans are Jews who live in the north but are not part of the 10 tribes exiled from that region by the Assyrians in 722 BCE. When the southern Judeans came back from their later Babylonian exile, they did not view the Samaritans as proper Jews; when the Jerusalem Temple was reestablished, the Samaritans constructed their own temple at Mount Gerizim, circa 500 BCE, where Joshua built an altar after the Israelites conquered Jericho.

When Jesus is in the area of Mount Gerizim, he stops at a well to rest while his disciples head to town to get food. There he meets the Samaritan Woman. He asks her for some water. She is surprised by the request and comments on how the two Jewish groups do not get along. "How is it that you, a Jew, ask a drink of me, a woman of Samaria?" The pair start to discuss faith, and Jesus describes to her the difference between water drawn each day from a well and the idea of living water, which brings eternal life. "Those who drink of the water that I will give them will never be thirsty," he tells her. "The water that I will give will become in them a spring of water gushing up to eternal life." He also explains how prayer should be done "in spirit and truth."

Soon the disciples return, and they are astonished that Jesus is talking with a Samaritan woman. The woman is moved by what Jesus says, and, leaving her water jar behind, she goes to the town and tells her neighbors to come and see him, helping to spread his ideas. ▪

DAILY LIFE

Even with God's help, life in Ancient Israel was hard. Women tended vegetable gardens, helped their husbands in the fields, raised children, and gathered water at wells. Their waking hours were largely passed preparing food, including special meals for the Sabbath and holidays. But these women were crucial to the development of the Jewish religion. While many of the 613 commandments in the Torah deal with sacrifices—which were held in Jerusalem and didn't relate to most Jews' daily lives—religious life centered in the home. "If you were living in Galilee you were not going to Jerusalem; maybe once in your lifetime if you were lucky," says Duke's Carol Meyers. "It was a long trip and it was dangerous." Women, who oversaw household religious practices, played a key role. It was up to mothers to pass on to their children the prayers and histories they knew from their own mothers and grandmothers.

A GROVE OF ALMOND TREES IN a field near the hills of Samaria, opposite. The well of the Samaritans, this page, where local women at the turn of the last century gathered water, as their ancestors before them would have.

MARY & MARTHA OF BETHANY
Miracle-Seeking Sisters

SHORTLY BEFORE JESUS'S CRUCIFIXION, he pays a visit to friends of his, sisters Mary and Martha and their brother, Lazarus. As Martha busily prepares a meal, Mary sits at Jesus's feet, listening to teachings from him. This annoys Martha, who complains to Jesus that while she is doing all the work, her sister is able to sit and relax. Jesus responds, "Martha, Martha, you are worried and distracted by many things; there is need of only one thing. Mary has chosen the better part, which will not be taken away from her."

As Mary listens, she spreads perfume on Jesus's feet. She then dries them with her hair. This act of respect calls to mind the anointing ceremony used for the Israelite rulers; Mary is seen to be designating Jesus as the messianic king.

Jesus and his disciples then start out for Jerusalem to celebrate the holiday of Passover. After they have left, Lazarus becomes sick, and a frantic Mary and Martha send word to Jesus to return to Bethany. But by the time he arrives, Lazarus has died and been lying in the tomb for four days. Martha implores Jesus to help. He tells her, "I am the resurrection and the life. Those who believe in me, even though they die, will live, and everyone who lives and believes in me will never die." When he asks her if she believes him, she replies, "Yes, Lord, I believe that you are the Messiah, the Son of God."

They then take Jesus to the tomb. The large stone blocking it is moved away. Jesus walks up to the entrance and calls out, "Lazarus, come out!" The recently deceased friend emerges, still wrapped in his burial clothes. ∎

MARY OF BETHANY LISTENS TO JESUS while her sister, Martha, does the housework, seen in a painting by Herbert Gustave Schmalz, opposite. Jesus returned to Bethany following the death of Lazarus. The book of John reveals that he went to his friend's tomb and called, "'Lazarus, come out!' The dead man came out," as depicted here by the 16th-century painter Juan de Flandes.

SALOME'S DANCE—SEEN HERE in *Herod's Birthday Feast* by the English painter Edward Armitage—so beguiled her stepfather, Herod Antipas, that he promised to give her whatever she asked for. She demanded the head of John the Baptist.

SALOME
The Bewitching Dancer

JOHN THE BAPTIST IS APPALLED WHEN he learns that Princess Herodias has divorced Herod Philip and married his half brother Herod Antipas. John denounces Herodias for violating Jewish law. To speak out against someone so powerful, though, has serious repercussions, and Herodias convinces her new husband, Herod Antipas, to toss John in jail. Even so, Antipas is not inclined to do more to punish John the Baptist, because, as Mark tells us, "Herod feared John, knowing that he was a righteous and holy man."

When a birthday banquet is held for Antipas at his palatial home at Machaerus, he invites his courtiers, as well as officers and leaders of Galilee. At the celebration, Herodias's daughter, Salome, dances for her stepfather. He is so taken by her performance that he says to her, "Whatever you ask me, I will give you, even half of my kingdom." Salome says to her mother, "What should I ask for?" Herodias says, "The head of John the baptizer." Salome dutifully passes along the request.

While the idea disturbs Antipas, he feels that he cannot renege on his promise, and sends an order to the soldier of the guard, who brings John's head on a platter and gives it to the girl. Pleased, Salome presents it to her mother.

This murderous incident has been a popular topic for many artists, from Renaissance painters to Oscar Wilde. But not every representation has stuck to the source material: Though Richard Strauss's operatic take on the story famously contains a seductive "Dance of the Seven Veils," there is no biblical reference that Salome ever performed that sort of a dance for Antipas. ∎

ON THE PAGE OPPOSITE, ` Salome holds John the Baptist's head in a painting by the 17th-century Italian artist Guido Reni. This page: The ruins of Herod's palace, Machaerus, where Salome danced. The structure is located to the east of the Dead Sea, and was built in about 90 BCE, during the Hasmonean dynasty of the Maccabees prior to Roman rule.

MARY MAGDALENE
The Faithful Follower

ONE OF THE PLACES TO WHICH JESUS travels during the years of his ministry is Magdala, a prosperous fishing community on the northwest side of the Sea of Galilee that is home to Mary Magdalene. When she is first mentioned in the books of Mark and Luke, Jesus has freed her of "seven demons," which could possibly be a physical disorder such as epilepsy that was believed to be caused by evil spirits. Saved from her tormentors, Mary becomes one of a number of women who follow Jesus. During her time with Jesus, Mary becomes one of his most faithful followers, supporting him with her own resources, and she is with him when he is crucified.

After Jesus's body is set in a newly carved tomb, Mary is one of the women who comes with spices and ointments to prepare his body for burial. A stone had been placed in front of the burial space, yet when they arrive they find it has been moved. Mary sees that the tomb is empty, and runs to tell the others. The disciples examine the space and discover there only the linen cloth in which Jesus had been wrapped. Not understanding what has happened, they

all return home—except Mary.

As she bends over to look inside, she sees two angels, who ask her, "Woman, why are you weeping?" She replies, "They have taken away my Lord, and I do not know where they have laid him." As she says this, she turns around, and sees Jesus. At first Mary does not realize that it is he. He too asks why she is crying. She asks what happened to Jesus's body, and he then responds, "Mary!" Realizing who he is, she cries out to her teacher, and Jesus informs her that he is ascending to heaven. Mary runs to the others to announce, "I have seen the Lord."

Mary thus is the first to reveal the glorious news of Christ's resurrection. Yet, while she is one of his most dedicated believers, Mary has often been unfairly branded as sinful and wrongly portrayed as Jesus's wife or as a prostitute, though nothing of the sort is mentioned in the Gospels. As early as the 3rd century she becomes wrongly associated with a different "sinner" mentioned in Luke who bathes Jesus's feet. Pope Gregory I even called her a "fallen woman." It was not until 1969 that the Catholic Church would declare that Mary was not the "sinful woman." ∎

A PORTRAIT OF MARY
Magdalene by the Florentine artist Piero di Cosimo, opposite. This page, *The Morning of the Resurrection* by the British painter Edward Burne-Jones, which depicts the disciple's arrival at the empty tomb, where she encounters two angels and the resurrected Christ.

In Her Honor

The Church of St. Mary Magdalene, with its seven gilded onion domes, stands on the western side of Jerusalem's Mount of Olives. Czar Alexander III of Russia had it built in 1888 in memory of his mother, Empress Maria Alexandrovna, who had Mary as her patron saint.

PRISCILLA
Messenger of Christ's Word

PRISCILLA AND HER HUSBAND, AQUILA, work as tentmakers. While it is a good way to make a living, their main purpose in life is spreading the word about Christ. The couple are considered two of the 70 disciples mentioned in the book of Acts, whom Jesus dispatches to reveal the word. They are successful proselytizers, and in the New Testament Priscilla is usually mentioned first, a sign that she is the more active promoter in church activities.

The couple had lived in Rome, but were forced to leave when Emperor Claudius expelled the Jews. They then head to Corinth and soon on to Ephesus, where they work with the Apostle Paul and train the missionary Apollos. Paul clearly relies on their support and protection, and praises them in the book of Romans, describing them as "Priscilla and Aquila, who work with me in Christ Jesus, and who risked their necks for my life."

After Paul leaves Ephesus, the couple run a church out of their home there. They seem to have then headed back to Rome, where they set up another church. Legend has it that Priscilla is the real writer behind the Epistle to the Hebrews, which sought to encourage the belief of the faithful. ∎

PRISCILLA SPREADING THE word about Christ in a painting, opposite, by Harold Copping. This page: The remains of the Church of St. Mary in Ephesus, Turkey. It was at the Council of Ephesus in 431 that the Church approved the first of four dogmas associated with Mary and proclaimed her the *Theotokos*, the Mother of God.

THECLA
Brave Believer

LIFE CAN PROVE DEADLY FOR THOSE who embrace Christ. Case in point: a woman named Thecla, who lives in Iconium in Turkey and is betrothed to Thamyris. When she hears Paul preaching, she becomes transfixed by his message and seeks to join his movement. To stop the apostle from taking his wife away, Thamyris gets Paul tossed into jail. Undeterred, Thecla uses her jewelry to free him. But a charge of sorcery is placed on Paul. At the same time, the townspeople decide to burn Thecla at the stake. But though the blaze encircles her, she does not burn. The sky then opens, and rain drenches the flames.

Thecla soon sets off with Paul. Yet when they arrive in Antioch, the city magistrate tries to rape her. Thecla fights back and humiliates the leader, after which she is condemned to be eaten by wild beasts. Her captors set her in an arena with a lion. But there the beast simply licks her feet. Other animals are sent in to devour her, and Thecla jumps into a pit of water in order to baptize herself. She is not aware, though, that the pool is filled with man-eating seals. Fortunately, at that moment, lightning strikes the water, killing the seals while leaving her unscathed. As more animals try to attack her, women in the audience toss flowers and perfume into the arena, causing the beasts to be hypnotized and stopping the assault.

Saved, Thecla converts the faithful. A benefactor gives her money to travel, and when she meets up with Paul, he recognizes the depth of her faith. "Go," he tells her, "and teach the Word of God."

For her good work, Thecla is venerated throughout the Christian world. She is the first female martyr and one of the most popular saints. ■

IN THE 1750s, GIOVANNI BATTISTA Tiepolo created *St. Thecla Freeing Este from the Plague* for the altarpiece of the cathedral at Este, Italy. It commemorates the plague of 1629–1631, which killed some 280,000 people throughout northern Italy, and which citizens believe was stopped through the intercession of Saint Thecla.

Photo Credits

"She opens her mouth with wisdom, and the
teaching of kindness is on her tongue."

PROVERBS, 31:26

THE INVENTOR JOHANNES GUTENBERG
lived in Mainz, Germany, and originated
the method of movable type. His creation,
which made possible the mass production
of books, such as this Bible from 1455,
revolutionized printing, and the world